D0884204

MEET BUSTER POSEY

Baseball's Superstar Catcher

Ethan Edwards

PowerKiDS
press
New York

Published in 2014 by The Rosen Publishing Group, Inc.
29 East 21st Street, New York, NY 10010

Copyright © 2014 by The Rosen Publishing Group, Inc.

First Edition

Editor: Jennifer Way and Joshua Shadowens
Book Design: Greg Tucker
Book Layout: Joe Carney
Photo Research: Katie Stryker

Photo Credits: Cover, pp. 1, 13, 16, 18, 20, 21, 27, 30 Brad Mangin/Getty Images; p. 5 Kevin Hill Illustration/ Shutterstock.com; p. 7 Thearon W. Henderson/Getty Images; p. 8 Photo Works/Shutterstock.com; p. 9 Jason O. Watson/Getty Images; p. 10 Raleigh News & Observer/McClatchy-Tribune/Getty Images; p. 12 Chris McGrath/ Getty Images; p. 14 Sacramento Bee/McClatchy-Tribune/Getty Images; pp. 17, 25, 27, 29 Ezra Shaw/Getty Images; pp. 19, 22, 26 Brad Mangin/Major League Baseball/Getty Images; p. 24 Jed Jacobsohn/ Getty Images.

Library of Congress Cataloging-in-Publication Data

Edwards, Ethan, author.
 Meet Buster Posey : baseball's superstar catcher / by Ethan Edwards. — 1st ed.
     pages cm. — (All-star players)
 Includes index.
 ISBN 978-1-4777-2915-1 (library) — ISBN 978-1-4777-3004-1 (pbk.) —
ISBN 978-1-4777-3075-1 (6-pack)
1. Posey, Buster, 1987-—Juvenile literature. 2. Baseball players—United States—Biography—Juvenile literature.
3. Catchers (Baseball)—United States—Biography—Juvenile literature. I. Title.
GV865.P676E39 2013
 796.357092—dc23
 [B]
                                      2013022324

Manufactured in the United States of America

CPSIA Compliance Information: Batch #W14PK2: For Further Information contact Rosen Publishing, New York, New York at 1-800-237-9932

Contents

A Star Is Born

It took only three seasons for Buster Posey to become one of the biggest stars in **Major League Baseball**. He had to sit out for most of his second season with an **injury**. This means that Posey accomplished more in two seasons than most ballplayers do in their entire careers.

Posey is the catcher for the San Francisco Giants. Sometimes he plays first base. While Posey is a great catcher, he is especially known for his hitting. He is already one of the best Giants of all time. He may go down in history as the all-time best catcher in baseball.

All-Star Facts

Posey's favorite television show is *Swamp People*.

Here Buster Posey is practicing his catching at the Giants' spring training in Scottsdale, Arizona. Spring training helps get players ready for the upcoming season.

Call Him Buster

Buster Posey was born on March 27, 1987, in Leesburg, Georgia. He is the oldest of four siblings. He has two brothers and a sister. Buster is just a nickname. His real name is Gerald Dempsey Posey III. His father was nicknamed Buster, so he passed both his name and his nickname on to his son.

Buster played baseball for his high-school team, and he quickly became famous as the best player in Georgia. Baseball **scouts** watched him closely during his junior year, when he collected 46 **runs batted in**, or RBIs, and finished the season with a **batting average** of .544. Buster was not only a good hitter, but he was also an excellent pitcher. Players from other high-school teams hated batting against him. As a pitcher, he did not lose a single game in his senior year. That same year, Buster set a school record when he hit 14 **home runs**. He was a great student, too. He got almost all As and graduated third in his class.

Posey's batting average in 2012 was .336 with 103 RBIs.

Here Posey has removed his catcher's mask as he takes a break during a game.

Posey entered the 2005 Major League Baseball **Draft**. This is how MLB teams pick the best young players. The Los Angeles Angels of Anaheim eventually picked Posey, but he decided he was not ready for **professional** baseball yet. He decided to go to college at Florida State, where he could continue his education while playing for the school's baseball team.

Choosing to play baseball in college before turning pro gave Posey time to develop his batting skills.

Going to college proved a wise decision for Posey's baseball career. He learned a lot playing for the Florida State Seminoles, including how to play the position that would make him famous. Until he got to college, Posey had never been a catcher. He had always pitched or played **shortstop**. The Seminoles' coach decided to try playing Posey at catcher during his sophomore, or second, year. A good catcher uses hand signals to tell the pitcher what to throw for certain batters. Since Posey had been such a good pitcher, he also knew how to be a great catcher.

Posey was tagged out as he slid into second base in this Seminoles game against the University of North Carolina Tar Heels.

Posey studied finance at Florida State, and he remained a good student. He also played some of the best baseball of his life. Posey's junior year was simply amazing. His batting average was .463, and he also won the Johnny Bench Award. This annual award is given to the nation's top catcher at the college level.

Posey did not start out as a catcher. However, players sometimes change positions when they join a team that already has players in their position.

Posey demonstrated that he could play different positions well. This meant that he caught the interest of several teams during the 2008 draft.

He also won the Collegiate Baseball Player of the Year Award. In one very special game on May 12, 2008, Posey hit a **grand slam**. In the same game, his coach also asked him to take a turn playing all nine positions. Posey even pitched and struck out both batters that he faced. He was definitely ready for professional baseball now!

When Posey entered the draft in 2008, the magazine *Baseball America* called him the best new catcher. The San Francisco Giants picked Posey fifth overall, out of hundreds of players.

Unlike football and basketball, rising to the top level in baseball after being drafted takes patience. Players in other sports are often drafted and then begin playing for a major-league team immediately in the next season. Baseball is different. It might take players years of competing in the **minor leagues** before they are ready to join a major-league team.

Posey is sliding into second base in this 2009 game against the Atlanta Braves. Posey played in only seven games that year.

Posey (left) and pitcher Barry Zito (right) are discussing what to do next during a 2009 game against the Chicago Cubs.

The minor leagues are a system of teams in which MLB teams develop their young talent. Most minor-league players never make it to the majors. Making it to the majors was never in doubt for Posey.

He knew he would not have to play in the minors long. In fact, he played less than two seasons before the Giants called him up to the majors. Due to an injury to catcher Bengie Molina, Posey was called up to the majors on September 11, 2009. Unfortunately, Posey did not get a hit in that game. He went back to the minors at the end of the season, but he did not stay there for long.

Major-league players often spend a few seasons in the minors before they are called up. Unlike Posey, most players will not rise all the way to the majors.

Winning It All as a Rookie

Most **rookies** are not stars immediately. Even the best rookies need time to adapt to playing the game against the greatest players in the world. Once again, Posey proved himself immediately. The Giants called him up from the minors again in May 2010, and this time he was more than ready.

On May 29, he played first base against the Arizona Diamondbacks. He got three hits and drove in three runs. Less than two weeks later, he hit his first major-league home run.

Posey hit 18 home runs in the 2010 season.

Here Posey is playing first base against the Arizona Diamondbacks on May 29, 2010.

Posey got the chance to be the Giants' full-time catcher when the team traded Molina away later that summer. In June and July of that season, Posey put together one of the longest hitting streaks in the history of baseball. He had a hit in 21 straight games. It was the second-longest hitting streak for a rookie ever.

Posey hugs 1975 Rookie of the Year John Montefusco as he receives the honor for 2010.

Posey finished his rookie season batting .305 with 67 RBIs. He was named the National League Rookie of the Year, but he was not finished winning awards. The Giants played well enough to make the **postseason**. Posey helped his team through each round. Then they faced the Texas Rangers in the World Series. The World Series is baseball's championship. Most players never get a World Series ring, let alone during their rookie seasons. Posey batted .300 and hit one home run in the series, and the Giants won. He got his first ring. Not bad for a rookie!

Winning It All Again!

Giants fans were eager to see what Posey did in his second season. Unfortunately, he played only 45 games because of an injury. On May 25, Florida Marlin Scott Cousins was running to home plate and crashed into Posey as he was trying to score. He broke Posey's lower leg when he hit him. Posey was out for the rest of the 2011 season. There was even a chance that the injury would end his career.

Many Giants fans believed the play in which Posey was injured was dirty, or unsportsmanlike. Some were angry with Cousins and even sent him death threats in the mail. Posey understood why fans were angry, but he spoke up for Cousins and told fans not to blame him. Posey worked hard so that he could return to the Giants for the 2012 season.

During the 2012 season, Posey had 520 at bats.

23

Players receive special rings when their team wins the World Series. Here Posey is receiving his ring for the Giants' 2010 World Series win.

The time off did not make Posey rusty. He had an excellent rookie season in 2010. In 2012, he had one of the best seasons of any catcher in baseball history. He finished the season with a batting average of .354, which was better than any other player that year. He won the batting title and was voted the National League's Most Valuable Player, or MVP. Baseball writers vote for the MVPs. The award means that the winning player did more to help his team than any other player in the league.

Here is Posey catching during Game Six of the 2012 National League Championship Series. The Giants won this game and went on to play in and win the 2012 World Series.

Posey helped the Giants reach the World Series again. This time they faced the Detroit Tigers and beat them easily, earning the Giants another World Series win.

All-Star Facts

At 23 years old, Posey was the youngest Giant to hit a home run during the World Series.

Posey is known for his leadership on the field. He is known for these same qualities off the field. He devotes himself to raising his family. Posey married in 2009. His wife, Kristin, was his high-school girlfriend. Buster and Kristin became the proud parents of **fraternal twins** in 2011. The twins are a boy named Lee and a girl named Addison.

Posey hit 24 home runs in the 2012 season. That was the most of anyone on the San Francisco Giants.

All-Star Facts

One charity that Posey has given thousands of dollars and lent his support to is called 19 for Life. This charity raises money to help children with serious illnesses.

The city of San Francisco held a victory parade for the San Francisco Giants after they won the 2012 World Series.

In 2013, the San Francisco Giants awarded Posey the biggest contract in the team's history. He would earn hundreds of millions of dollars. As part of this generous deal, Posey agreed to donate at least $50,000 each year to different **charities**.

Buster Posey's wife, Kristin, is holding their daughter, Addison. His mother is holding his son, Lee. His father is on the right.

One of the Greatest

Most baseball players never achieve in their careers what Buster Posey has in a very short time. Giants fans love him, and even fans from other teams respect him as one of the best in the game. Posey helped his team win two World Series in three seasons, so his fans believe that he can do anything.

Here Posey is tagging out San Diego Padre Mark Kotsay in a 2013 game.

Some athletes love to brag. Posey is quiet. He brags with his bat and with his records. Most baseball players improve over time. If that holds true, Buster Posey might one day be the best catcher who ever lived. He has already made baseball history. It will be fun to follow his career.

Stat Sheet

Team: San Francisco Giants
Position: Catcher and
   first baseman
Bats: Right
Uniform Number: 28
Born: March 27, 1989
Height: 6 feet 1 inch (1.85 m)
Weight: 220 pounds (100 kg)

Year	Team	Batting Average	RBIs	Home Runs
2009	San Francisco Giants	.118	0	0
2010	San Francisco Giants	.305	67	18
2011	San Francisco Giants	.284	21	4
2012	San Francisco Giants	.336	103	24

Glossary

batting average (BA-ting A-veh-rij) A number that measures how good a hitter is. It is the number of hits divided by at bats.

charities (CHER-uh-teez) Groups that give help to the needy.

draft (DRAFT) The selection of people for a special purpose.

fraternal twins (fruh-TER-nul TWINZ) Two babies who are born to one mother at the same time but who come from two different eggs.

grand slam (GRAND SLAM) A home run that is hit when the bases are loaded. This earns a team four runs and is the most it is possible for a team to score on one play.

home runs (HOHM RUNZ) Hits in which the batter touches all the bases and scores a run.

injury (INJ-ree) Physical harm or hurt done to a person.

Major League Baseball (MAY-jur LEEG BAYS-bawl) The top group of baseball teams in the United States.

minor leagues (MY-nur LEEGZ) Groups of teams on which players play before they are good enough for the next level.

postseason (pohst-SEE-zun) Games played after the regular season.

professional (pruh-FESH-nul) Having players who are paid.

rookies (RU-keez) New major-league players.

runs batted in (RUNZ BAT-ed IN) When a player's at bat results in runs being scored, usually abbreviated RBIs.

scouts (SKOWTS) People who help sports teams find new, young players.

shortstop (SHORT-stop) The baseball player who stands between second and third base.

Index

Websites

Due to the changing nature of Internet links, PowerKids Press has developed an online list of websites related to the subject of this book. This site is updated regularly. Please use this link to access the list: www.powerkidslinks.com/asp/posey/